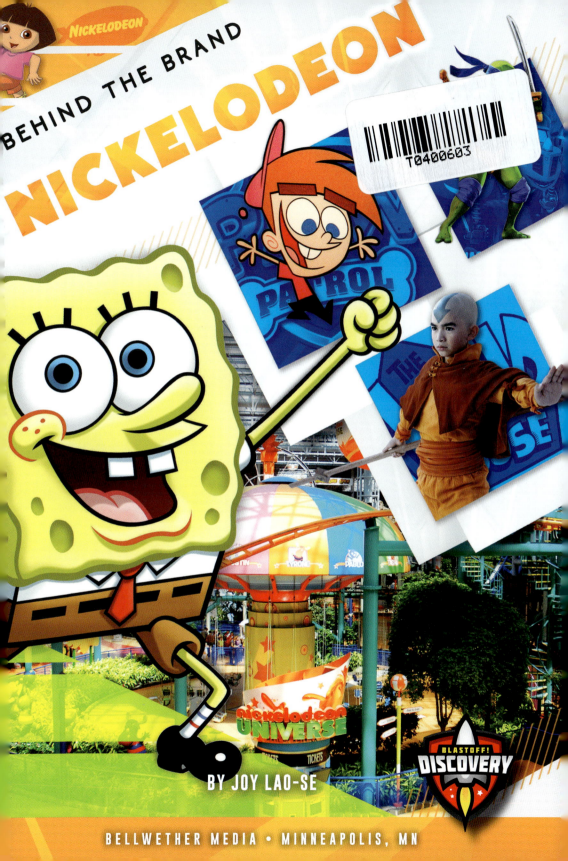

BEHIND THE BRAND

NICKELODEON

BY JOY LAO-SE

BELLWETHER MEDIA • MINNEAPOLIS, MN

Blastoff! Discovery launches a new mission: reading to learn. Filled with facts and features, each book offers you an exciting new world to explore!

BLASTOFF! UNIVERSE

BLASTOFF! Beginners — GRADE K

BLASTOFF! READERS — GRADES 1-3

DISCOVERY — GRADE 4

This edition first published in 2025 by Bellwether Media, Inc.

Library of Congress Cataloging-in-Publication Data

LC record for Nickelodeon available at: https://lccn.loc.gov/2024046798

Editor: Betsy Rathburn   Series Designer: Andrea Schneider   Book Designer: Josh Brink

Printed in the United States of America, North Mankato, MN.

TABLE OF
CONTENTS

SATURDAY MORNING TELEVISION

HENRY DANGER

It is Saturday! A girl wakes up and runs to the living room with her brother. No school means it is time to watch TV. They flip through Nickelodeon channels to see what is on.

On TeenNick, they see Henry Hart busy saving the world in *Henry Danger*. On Nick Jr., Ryder and his crew of dogs are on a mission in *PAW Patrol*. Eventually, the siblings decide to watch *SpongeBob Squarepants*. The kids love watching Nickelodeon shows!

SPONGEBOB SQUAREPANTS

PAW PATROL

PINWHEEL PROGRAMMING

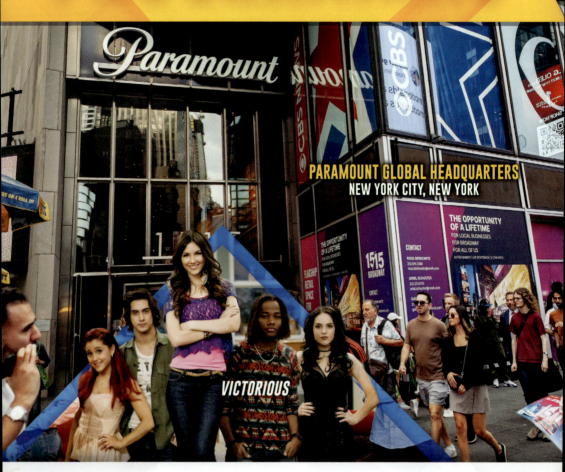

PARAMOUNT GLOBAL HEADQUARTERS
NEW YORK CITY, NEW YORK

VICTORIOUS

Nickelodeon, or Nick, is a TV **network** owned by a company called Paramount Global. Its **headquarters** is in New York City, New York. The **brand** also includes other channels such as TeenNick and Nick Jr. Nick is famous for its original cartoons like *SpongeBob SquarePants* and *Rugrats*. The Teenage Mutant Ninja Turtles and other **animated** characters are popular, too. Nick also makes **live-action** shows such as *Victorious*.

Outside of TV shows, there are many ways to enjoy Nick. The company makes movies and video games based on its most popular characters. There are even Nickelodeon theme parks!

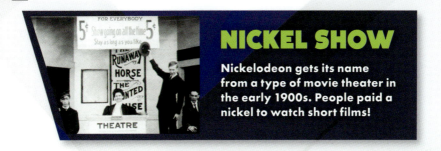

NICKEL SHOW

Nickelodeon gets its name from a type of movie theater in the early 1900s. People paid a nickel to watch short films!

PARAMOUNT GLOBAL HEADQUARTERS

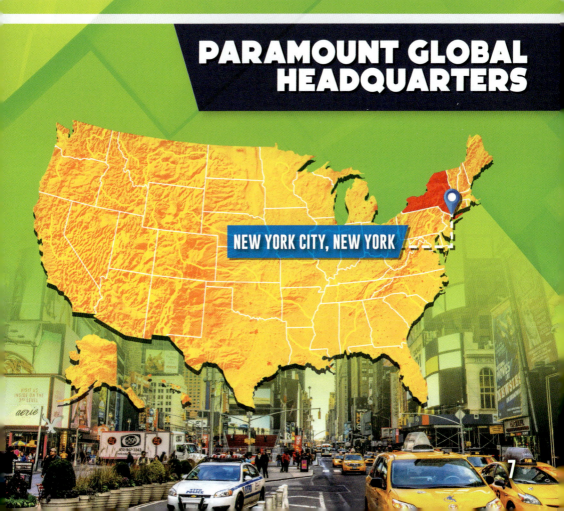

NEW YORK CITY, NEW YORK

Nickelodeon began on December 1, 1977. It was originally called Pinwheel. It was named after a show created by Vivian Horner. The show aired in Columbus, Ohio. Its popularity led to a new network. *Pinwheel* was the first show to air on the Pinwheel network.

PINWHEEL

NICKELODEON TIMELINE

1977
The children's show *Pinwheel* begins, inspiring a TV network with the same name

1990
Nickelodeon Studios opens at Universal Studios in Florida

1979
Pinwheel is renamed Nickelodeon and becomes a nationwide network

2001
The Fairly OddParents first airs

2023
Teenage Mutant Ninja Turtles: Mutant Mayhem is released

2007
iCarly first airs

1991
Nickelodeon airs its first original Nicktoons

1988
Nick Jr. begins

1999
SpongeBob SquarePants first airs

2010
Victorious first airs

In time, many cartoons were added. This included short cartoons from around the world. The network did not include **commercials**. Over time, its popularity grew. In 1979, Pinwheel was renamed Nickelodeon. It became available across the United States!

9

CAST OF *YOU CAN'T DO THAT ON TELEVISION*

Around this time, there were no other channels for children. Nick called itself the first children's network. In 1979, *You Can't Do That on Television* began airing. It was a comedy show that included jokes and **skits**. It also showed Nick's green slime for the first time!

SLIME RECIPE

Nickelodeon's famous slime has had many ingredients over the years. It has included baby shampoo, applesauce, oatmeal, and Jell-O. Its famous coloring comes from green food dye!

The show enjoyed some success. But the network made little money. In the 1980s, Nick started airing commercials to earn more money. Around the same time, Geraldine Laybourne took over as Nick's president. Geraldine helped the network grow. She made sure it kept its focus on what kids would enjoy.

GERALDINE LAYBOURNE

BORN May 19, 1947

ROLE President of Nickelodeon from 1984 to 1996

ACCOMPLISHMENTS

Helped the Nickelodeon brand grow

11

Despite the changes, Nick still struggled with money. Viewership was not as high as leaders wanted. To gain more viewers, the network got a new song and **logo**. The logo's playful color and shape were made to appeal to kids.

EARLY NICKELODEON LOGO

DOUBLE DARE

DORA THE EXPLORER

Nick also added more shows to its lineup. *Double Dare* began in 1986. Two teams of kids had to answer trivia questions and do messy challenges. Nick Jr. began in 1988. It aired shows for young kids in the morning. In time, popular shows such as *Dora the Explorer* and *PAW Patrol* were introduced.

MORNING AND NIGHT

In 1985, Nick at Nite began. Reruns of older shows aired in the evenings.

In the 1990s, many new game shows aired on Nick. In *Legends of the Hidden Temple*, kids competed in **obstacle courses**. In *Figure It Out*, actors asked questions to guess a kid's hidden talent.

SCARY SUCCESS!

Are You Afraid of the Dark? aired until 1996. But many fans missed it. Nick brought it back in 1999 and 2019!

FIGURE IT OUT

Jessica

CAST OF *ALL THAT*

THE AMANDA SHOW

Other live-action shows were also added to the lineup. *Are You Afraid of the Dark?* began in 1990. Kids shared scary ghost stories. *All That* began airing in 1994. Actors did funny skits. Several **spin-offs** were based on *All That* skits. *Kenan & Kel* and *The Amanda Show* were popular.

NICKTOONS AND MORE

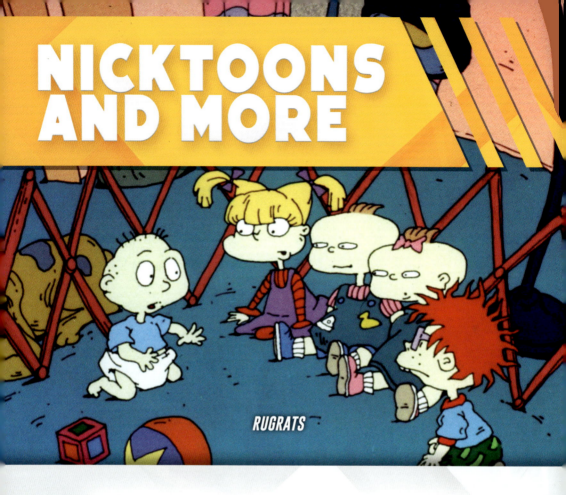

RUGRATS

In 1991, Nick began airing its first original cartoons. They were called Nicktoons. *Doug* followed a boy and his friends. *Rugrats* was about the adventures of a group of babies. *The Ren & Stimpy Show* was about a goofy cat and dog. Some people thought the humor in *The Ren & Stimpy Show* was not appropriate for kids. But many kids loved it.

READ ALL ABOUT IT!

The first *Nickelodeon Magazine* was released in 1990. It included puzzles, short comics, and more. The magazine printed until 2009!

Monster-Size Scary Issue: Read It If You DARE!

NICKELODEON

Sabrina TAKES TV BY STORM

More Nicktoons followed. In 1996, *Hey Arnold!* aired. It was about a boy and his friends. In 1998, *The Wild Thornberrys* followed a girl who could talk to animals. By this time, Nick was one of the top cable channels!

EARLY NICKTOONS

1991 DOUG

1991 THE REN & STIMPY SHOW

1991 RUGRATS

1994 AAAHH!!! REAL MONSTERS

1996 HEY ARNOLD!

1997 THE ANGRY BEAVERS

1998 THE WILD THORNBERRYS

Even more Nicktoon success followed. In 1999, Nick aired the first episode of *SpongeBob SquarePants*. Viewers loved the goofy show about a loveable sponge and his friends. The show gained over 55 million viewers by 2002. Two years later, *The SpongeBob SquarePants Movie* came out. It earned over $140 million.

18

In 2015, *The SpongeBob Movie: Sponge Out of Water* earned over $325 million! The third SpongeBob movie, *The SpongeBob Movie: Sponge on the Run* came out in 2020. It earned less. But many still love this popular Nick **mascot**!

MORE SPONGEBOB

More SpongeBob movies are in the works! Creators began making the fourth movie in 2022. It is called *The SpongeBob Movie: Search for SquarePants.*

THE SPONGEBOB MOVIE: SPONGE OUT OF WATER

Other new shows followed. *The Fairly OddParents* began in 2001. It follows a boy whose wishes are granted by two fairy godparents. It aired for ten seasons! In 2005, *Avatar: The Last Airbender* first aired. A young boy learns to control the four elements. Viewers loved it. It won many awards!

FAVORITE NICKTOON CHARACTERS

SPONGEBOB SQUAREPANTS

Show: *SpongeBob SquarePants*

AANG

Show: *Avatar: The Last Airbender*

TIMMY TURNER

Show: *The Fairly OddParents*

TOMMY PICKLES

Show: *Rugrats*

REGGIE ROCKET

Show: *Rocket Power*

ELIZA THORNBERRY

Show: *The Wild Thornberrys*

SAM PUCKETT

CAST OF *BIG TIME RUSH*

Nick introduced new live-action shows, too. *iCarly* first aired in 2007. It follows a girl who hosts her own internet show. *Big Time Rush* and *Victorious* both feature musical performances. *Henry Danger* follows a boy who becomes a superhero's sidekick! Nick continues to add fun new shows!

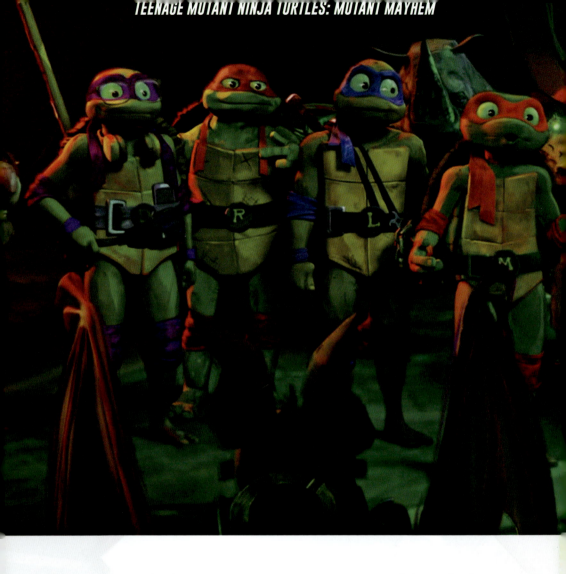

Nick also creates movies. In 2009, Nick bought the **rights** to the Teenage Mutant Ninja Turtles **franchise**. Several movies followed. In 2023, *Teenage Mutant Ninja Turtles: Mutant Mayhem* came out. Many liked its animation style. It got good reviews!

Movies based on other Nick characters have also been released. In 2010, *The Last Airbender* came out. It is a live-action version of the popular Nicktoon *Avatar: The Last Airbender*. In 2019, *Dora and the Lost City of Gold* released. It was based on the *Dora the Explorer* cartoon. In 2021, the first PAW Patrol movie came out. Nick has many more movies planned!

NICK MOVIE EARNINGS

	YEAR	EARNINGS
THE LAST AIRBENDER	2010	$319,713,881
THE SPONGEBOB MOVIE: SPONGE OUT OF WATER	2015	$325,186,032
DORA AND THE LOST CITY OF GOLD	2019	$120,597,108
PAW PATROL: THE MOVIE	2021	$144,327,371
TEENAGE MUTANT NINJA TURTLES: MUTANT MAYHEM	2023	$180,513,586

CARTOON COMMUNITY

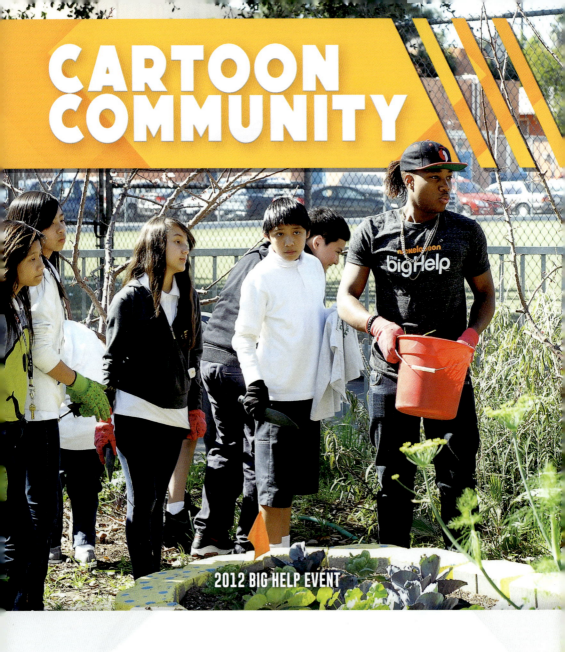

2012 BIG HELP EVENT

Nickelodeon gives back to the community. In 1991, it started a program called The Big Help. Nickelodeon helped kids rebuild local parks! The brand also helps people get food. In 2020, it **donated** $1 million to No Kid Hungry.

Nickelodeon is committed to helping in schools. In 2014, the company gave nearly 100 computers to a California school district. In 2020, the Nickelodeon School Partnership Program helped 275,000 kids across 200 schools. Nickelodeon provided resources for learning in subjects like science and reading.

GIVING BACK

$1 MILLION
GIVEN TO NO KID HUNGRY IN 2020

NEARLY 100
COMPUTERS GIVEN TO A CALIFORNIA SCHOOL DISTRICT IN 2014

275,000 KIDS
ACROSS 200 SCHOOLS REACHED BY NICKELODEON SCHOOL PARTNERSHIP PROGRAM IN 2020

FUN FOR FANS

NICKELODEON UNIVERSE
THEME PARK IN MINNESOTA

There are many ways for fans to enjoy the Nickelodeon brand. Fans can explore Nickelodeon **resorts** in Mexico and the Dominican Republic. Families enjoy water parks, pose on the orange carpet, and hang out with characters.

Nickelodeon Universe theme parks are also full of fun! One in Minnesota has rides based on *SpongeBob SquarePants*, *Dora the Explorer*, and other popular cartoons. In 2019, Nick opened its largest indoor park in New Jersey. The park covers over 350,000 square feet (32,516 square meters)!

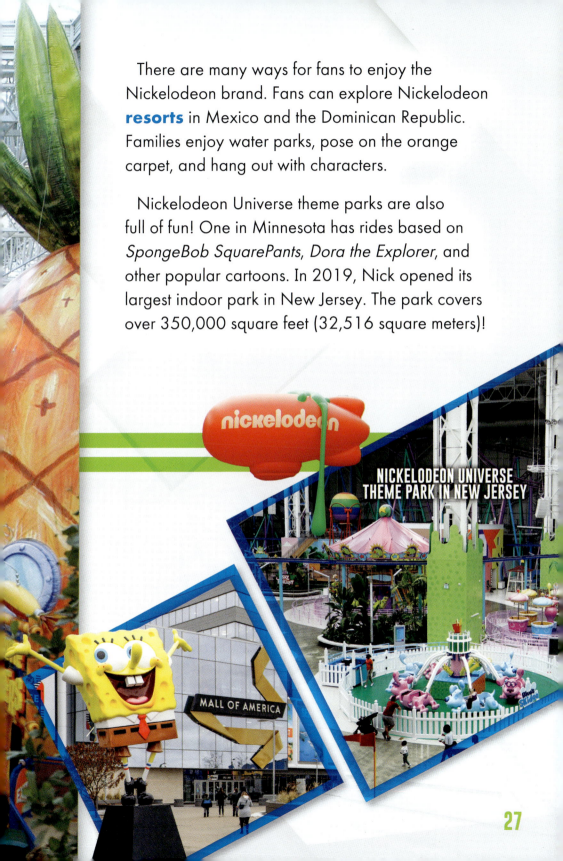

NICKELODEON UNIVERSE THEME PARK IN NEW JERSEY

MALL OF AMERICA

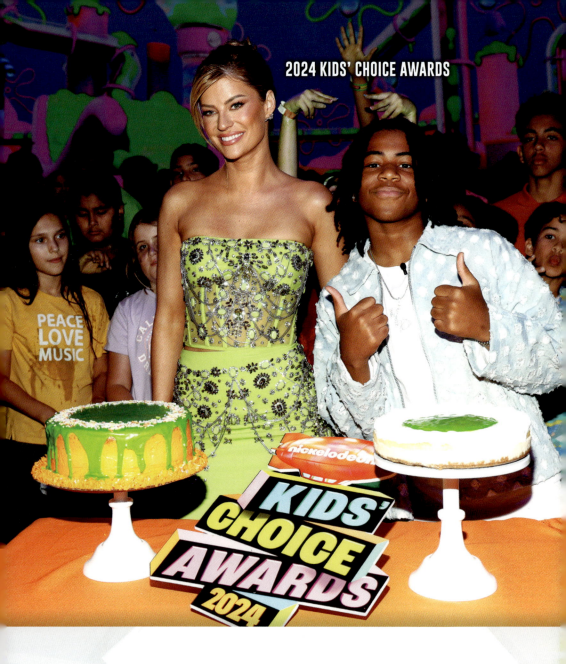

Each year, Nick holds the Kids' Choice Awards. This awards show honors the best actors, musical artists, shows, and more. Kids get to choose the winners! They vote for their favorites online. The winners are announced on TV!

Fans can also go to **conventions**. Comic-Con events let people meet creators and celebrate their favorite characters. In 2024, the first Splat Con was held in Los Angeles, California. It was an entirely fan-run event. Fans could meet actors from their favorite Nick shows, share fan art, and more. Nickelodeon inspires fun for fans of all ages!

KIDS' CHOICE AWARDS

WHAT IT IS

An awards show for fan favorites in categories like TV and movies

FIRST HELD

1987

WHEN IT HAPPENS

Once every year

WHERE IT HAPPENS

California

GLOSSARY

animated—made up of images that look as though they are moving

brand—a category of products all made by the same company

commercials—advertisements played on TV or radio; advertisements are public notices that tell people about products, services, or events.

conventions—events where fans of a subject meet

donated—gave money or other things to support a cause

franchise—a collection of books, movies, or other media that are related to one another

headquarters—a company's main office

live-action—filmed using real actors

logo—a symbol or design that identifies a brand or product

mascot—a character used as a symbol by a group or company

network—a company that provides television programming to many television stations

obstacle courses—courses that contain objects to be climbed, crawled under, or crossed

resorts—vacation spots that offer recreation, entertainment, and relaxation

rights—a legal claim to something

skits—short performances, usually comedy

spin-offs—movies, TV shows, or books that are based on other movies, TV shows, or books

TO LEARN MORE

AT THE LIBRARY

Grack, Rachel. *Movies From Then to Now*. Mankato, Minn.: Amicus, 2022.

Green, Sara. *Disney*. Minneapolis, Minn.: Bellwether Media, 2023.

Green, Sara. *The Television*. Minneapolis, Minn.: Bellwether Media, 2022.

ON THE WEB

FACTSURFER

Factsurfer.com gives you a safe, fun way to find more information.

1. Go to www.factsurfer.com.

2. Enter "Nickelodeon" into the search box and click 🔍.

3. Select your book cover to see a list of related content.

INDEX

The images in this book are reproduced through the courtesy of: Photo 12/ Alamy, front cover (SpongeBob SquarePants); James Kirkikis, front cover (Nickelodeon Universe); FlixPix/ Alamy, front cover (*Avatar: The Last Airbender*); Nickelodeon/ Wikipedia, front cover (*The Loud House*), pp. 12 (logo), 13 (Nick at Nite logo), 31 (blimp); Kim+5, front cover (Timmy Turner), p. 20 (Timmy Turner); chrisdorney, front cover (*PAW Patrol*); Sarunyu L, front cover (Teenage Mutant Ninja Turtle); cfg1978, front cover (*Blaze and the Monster Machines*); Mohan 0842, front cover (*Dora the Explorer*); Carrienelson1, front cover (logo); John Arehart, p. 2; Ritu Manoj Jethani, p. 3; Lopolo, pp. 4-5; Lisa Rose/ Nickelodeon/ Everett Collection, pp. 5 (*Henry Danger*), 6 (*Victorious*), 21 (*iCarly*); AJ Pics/ Alamy, pp. 5 (SpongeBob SquarePants), 13 (*Dora the Explorer*); Robert Kneschke/ Alamy, p. 5 (*PAW Patrol*); rblfmr, p. 6 (headquarters); American Stock Archive/ Getty Images, p. 7 (top); Luciano Mortula - LGM, p. 7 (New York City); Nickelodeon/ Everett Collection, pp. 8 (*Pinwheel*), 14 (*Figure It Out*); ViacomCBS/ Wikipedia, p. 9 (Nick Jr.); digitalreflections, p. 9 (*SpongeBob SquarePants*); Emerald Xiang Dianelle/ Wikipedia, p. 9 (Cosmo); Paramount+/ Wikipedia, p. 9 (*iCarly* logo); Christine McGlade/ Everett Collection, p. 10 (*You Can't Do That on Television*); Jimmie48 Photography, p. 10 (slime); TBM/ Alamy, pp. 11 (*Rugrats*), 17 (*Doug, Ren & Stimpy, Aaahh!!! Real Monsters*); AP Photo/ L.M. Otero/ AP Newsroom, p. 11 (Geraldine Laybourne); MTV/ Everett Collection, p. 12 (*Double Dare*); ozzichka, p. 12 (splatter); Jonathan Wenk/ Nickelodeon/ Everett Collection, p. 14 (*Are You Afraid of the Dark?*); Tollin/Robbins Prod./ Everett Collection, p. 15 (*All That*); Nickelodeon Network/ Everett Collection, pp. 15 (*The Amanda Show*), 16 (*Rugrats*); margonz_4071/ eBay, p. 16 (magazine); Album/ Alamy, pp. 17 (*Rugrats*), 20 (Aang, Tommy Pickles); Cinematic/ Alamy, p. 17 (*Hey Arnold!*); IFA Film, p. 17 (*The Angry Beavers*); Collection Christophel/ Alamy, pp. 17 (*The Wild Thornberrys*), 22 (*Teenage Mutant Ninja Turtles: Mutant Mayhem*); Entertainment Pictures/ Alamy, p. 18 (*The SpongeBob SquarePants Movie*); Gabe Ginsberg/ Getty Images, p. 19 (*Search for SquarePants*); TCD/Prod.DB/ Alamy, p. 19 (*Sponge Out of Water*); Zefry_Novizar, p. 20 (SpongeBob SquarePants); Cinematic Collection/ Alamy, p. 20 (Reggie Rocket, Eliza Thornberry); DFree, p. 21 (Big Time Rush); Jayson246, p. 23 (*Sponge Out of Water*); DatBot/ Wikipedia, p. 23 (*PAW Patrol*); Charley Gallay/ Getty Images, p. 24 (Big Help event); ElenaR, p. 25 (top); BearFotos, p. 25 (bottom left); Iren Moroz, p. 25 (bottom right); Dawn Vilella/ AP Newsroom, pp. 26-27; AaronP/Bauer-Griffin/ Getty Images, p. 27 (Mall of America); AP Photo/ Seth Wenig/ AP Newsroom, p. 27 (Nickelodeon Universe in New Jersey); Phillip Faraone/ Stringer/ Getty Images, p. 28 (2024 Kids' Choice Awards); VALERIE MACON/ AFP/ Getty Images, p. 29 (Kids' Choice Awards); Art_Gants, p. 31 (SpongeBob SquarePants).